# Weymouth and Melcombe Regis
## in old picture postcards volume 2

by Maureen Attwooll and Jack West

*European Library* ZALTBOMMEL/THE NETHERLANDS

**BACK IN TIME**

GB ISBN 90 288 6478 4 ⌣ ✗ ०।

© 1997 European Library – Zaltbommel/The Netherlands

# Introduction

The tradition of sending a postcard home has long been a feature of the seaside holiday. Today's gift shops display racks of bright views of azure skies and golden sands alongside souvenir mugs and tea towels, buckets and spades, Lilos, windbreaks and multi-coloured lettered rock. The first 'postcards' were sent through the post in this country in 1870 and by 1900 the picture postcard was firmly established as a popular means of communication and a collecting craze. The postcard album became a centrepiece in many homes and the message on the back of a card would often be 'another one for your collection' or 'have you got this view?'. Best of all for the Victorian and Edwardian holiday-makers who wanted to write home, the picture postcard cost only $^1/_2$d to send, half the cost of a letter!

Many of the pictures chosen for this book reflect 'seaside' Weymouth, but the town's holiday industry is of comparatively recent date – the first 'bathing houses' were established here in the 1740's and it was 1789 before Weymouth found real fame as King George III's favourite health and pleasure resort. Prosperity for the town's earlier inhabitants depended not on the sands and Bay, but on port trade through Weymouth Harbour. That continuing maritime link is illustrated in photographs of the harbour and its ships.

The modern resort and port of Weymouth has grown from what were originally two separate small communities at the mouth of the River Wey. Weymouth, the older of the two, was on the south side of the harbour, Melcombe (later Melcombe Regis), on the north. Ports of some standing, the pair became quarrelsome rivals as each sought to profit most from the ships using the harbour they had to share. The long history of rivalry and occasional violence was brought to an end in Queen Elizabeth I's reign, when the towns were virtually ordered to become the single Borough of Weymouth and Melcombe Regis in 1571. Co-operation between them was by no means immediate, but by the beginning of the seventeenth century most of the earlier differences had been overcome.

Port trade had always been subject to disruption by the actions of hostile raiders, pirates and the effects of foreign wars, but the 1640's brought more serious consequences when there was a period of fierce fighting within the town itself during the English Civil War. Much damage was caused to the harbour, its bridge and quays and to the morale of the inhabitants themselves, whose homes and businesses had suffered during the fray. Trade began again once the aftermath of war had been attended to, but there was no great resurgence of Weymouth as a port.

Fortunate, then, for Weymouth and other small coastal towns, that physicians in the first half of the 18th century began to promote sea water as a cure for all the ills of the age. (At first, not only to bathe in, but also to drink – gallon bottles of Weymouth sea water were sold, to be drunk 'a pint at a time'.) The first visitors began to arrive. One early and wealthy health-seeker was Ralph Allen, of Bath. His family's summer home was on the Weymouth side of the harbour and close to it the 'Assembly Rooms' opened and were later extended to accommodate and entertain the 'genteel company' who followed suit and sampled the health-giving properties of sea bathing. Gradually the resort became established and among the visitors in the 1760's was William Henry, 1st Duke of Gloucester and younger brother of King George III. More visits followed and the Duke decided to build himself a summer residence on the new 'seafront' in the town which had previously focused all its attention on the harbour. By now, the north, or Melcombe, side of the harbour was taking over as the centre for fashionable society. Gloucester Lodge and other buildings of the 1770's and 1780's which faced the Bay were the start of the modern Esplanade, an area previously considered to be the back of the town and of no importance.

Weymouth had everything it needed to succeed as the fashion for seabathing grew – soft, gently sloping sands and calm, sheltered waters in Weymouth Bay. King George III set the seal on its new prosperity when he arrived here in the summer of 1789, a monarch badly in need of rest and recuperation. Doctors of the day had been unable to identify the illness which had led them to diagnose the King as 'mad'. Poor King George was bled and blistered, straitjacketed and despaired of. When he eventually began to show signs of recovery it was in spite of, rather than because of, these harsh medical treatments. A long rest with sea bathing was to be his convalescence – and what better place to stay than Weymouth, where his brother's house was to serve as the King's holiday home during fourteen summers between 1789 and 1805. The result for the town was fame and fortune, for where the King went, society followed.

When King George III eventually became too frail to visit the seaside, the days of 'Royal Weymouth' came to an end, but the slight lessening of the holiday trade was quite short-lived. In 1840 the railway line to Dorchester opened and in 1857 the trains reached Weymouth, thus removing the only real obstacle to Weymouth's future as a successful seaside resort – its distance from the major towns and cities. Now there were new visitors to take the place of the wealthy Georgians who had spent leisurely weeks and even months by the sea. The railway companies brought cheap rail travel to the masses and Victorian holiday-makers began to pour into the town seeking reasonably-priced accommodation, entertainment and a chance to relax. The era of the family seaside holiday began in Victorian times and continues today, despite the lure of the guaranteed sunshine of a package tour abroad.

National postcard publishers produced many fine photographic views – well-known firms such as Raphael Tuck & Sons, Valentine & Sons and others are known for their scenes of town and village life. But it is the work of local photographers which predominates in this book – they were out and about taking pictures of lesser-known street scenes, local events and celebrations, and the occasional disaster. By 1907 there were at least fifteen commercial photographers in Weymouth and it is the work of these Edwardian postcard publishers which appears in the pages that follow – names such as W.G. Cox, H. Cumming, Edward Hitch, W.J. Masters, Weeks & Gimblett, Harry Wheeler and possibly the most prolific of all, Edwin H. Seward of Turton Street. A little later come the names of the twenties and after – W.H. Cumming, and the Herbert and Kestin families. A surprising number of early postcards, although obviously printed locally, bear no publisher's name at all.

This is our second selection of pictures of Weymouth in this series. We have captioned them using sources of information which we have collected and to which many people have contributed over the years, and we thank them all. Very special thanks go to Terry Gale, Brian Jackson, Bill Macey and Dennis Willes for the loan of postcards. For permission to reproduce photographs we are very grateful to Mrs. Ruth Lawrence for 'Herbert' photographs Nos. 25, 41, 45, 56, 63 and 107, to Mr. Tony Walden Biles for No. 110, to Mr. Edwin Kestin for C. and S. Kestin views Nos. 16, 42 and 65, to Mr. John Thompson for William Thompson's early photographs, Nos. 18 and 33, and to Judges Postcards Ltd. for No. 35 (© Photograph Judges Postcards Ltd., Hastings 01424 420919).

Most of the photographs selected date from the period 1900 to 1930, with one or two of earlier or later date which continue a particular story or recall something of historic interest which has disappeared in more recent times.

1 King Street, and a first sight of Weymouth for the many thousands of holiday-makers who streamed off packed trains arriving at Weymouth Railway Station in the days before the motor car took over as a more popular mode of family travel. The railway station entrance is on the left and a glance towards the Esplanade brings the Jubilee Clock into view. On the corner of King Street and Park Street stood Christchurch, an imposing design by architect Ewan Christian. Consecrated in 1874, it served a growing population at the northern end of Melcombe Regis parish, where reclaimed land, originally intended as a public park, was sold off and filled with the streets and houses of the Park District. By the 1930's the church had become redundant as a place of worship. It was demolished in 1956 and shops and flats (Garnet Court) now fill the site. The railway station was replaced by a new building in 1986.

2  Seen here on a wintry day in the early 1900's, Park Street was once intended to lead to the entrance gates of the proposed 'Royal Victoria Park', to be laid out on fifty acres of land reclaimed from Weymouth Backwater. The grandiose plans were beset by problems from the start and the park never materialised. In the 1850's the Great Western and London and South Western railway companies purchased part of the infilled area to bring lines and station buildings to the town, and the rest was sold off for building. Park Street then became quite an important commercial thoroughfare, linking the old and new developments in Melcombe and providing a shopping street for the growing number of hotels, boarding houses and pubs which grew up around the railway station. On the left-hand side of the photograph can be seen Weymouth Co-op's first premises in the town.

3 A closer view of Weymouth and District Co-operative Society's shop shown in the previous photograph. The building still exists today, on the corner of Park Street and Albert Street. The foundation of the Weymouth Co-op dates back to 1865 and this was the Society's first local shop. The early years of the twentieth century saw a great expansion of the Weymouth Society, with more branches opening in other parts of the Park District, and at Chapelhay, Westham, the town centre, Wyke and Portland, culminating in the opening of a purpose-built department store in Westham Road in 1926 (now renamed 'Living').

4   Just along Park Street, on the opposite side from the Co-op, was another business which was to expand rapidly following its foundation here in the early 1880's. Starting up as a 'General Draper and Wholesale Haberdasher', Mr. V.H. Bennett went on to become one of the town's leading citizens and its Mayor in 1918. He bought up and rebuilt a number of smaller shops around the junction of St. Thomas Street, Bond Street and St. Mary Street, gradually increasing the size of 'Bennetts Department Store'. The tall building in the background is the Victorian Queen's Hotel, which was completely rebuilt by brewers Eldridge Pope in 1939 to herald the arrival of the proposed new Weymouth Railway Station. In fact, the station did not materialise for another 47 years and then on a much smaller scale than the planned expansion of the Thirties.

Bennett's in Park Street is now the site of a 'Southern National' workshop.

5  Two Edwardian bicyclists make their way along West Parade towards its junction with Little George Street. These are unfamiliar locations today, as both streets have since been renamed. West Parade was the original name of Park Street, from its junction with Gloucester Street down to Westham Road, which was originally called Little George Street. A number of old properties on the left of the picture survive today, mostly converted to shops, although some buildings have given way to modern apartment blocks. On the opposite side of the street, graceful trees screen the large stone-gabled sheds of Betts' (later Webb Major's) timber yards.

The sheds were demolished in the 1980's and this cleared area between Park Street and Commercial Road is currently used as a car park.

6 Aerial photographs provide some striking views of the town and this one shows an unusually empty space in front of the King's Statue, an area where horse-drawn carriages and later motor charabancs, coaches and buses assembled, ready to take residents and visitors out and about. It is a fine day, the beach is crowded, so perhaps the trippers have left to enjoy a cream tea in the Dorset beauty spots. The background of this picture is of most interest – it shows the four huge timber sheds mentioned in the previous caption and also an adjacent wood pond which once ran right up to Gloucester Street – almost to the twin-spired Gloucester Street Congregational Church, seen on the right. The church was demolished in 1980. When the present Westham Bridge was completed in 1921, reclamation began of the area of water beyond Commercial Road on which Melcombe Regis Gardens were to be laid out. Some ground at the northern end had already been infilled when Melcombe Regis Station was built in 1909 to serve the Portland railway line.

WEYMOUTH.     SANDS

COPYRIGHT

7 A second aerial view takes us a little farther south and dates from about 1920. The shape of the pier had changed little since the mid-nineteenth century, apart from an extension into the Bay to provide a site for the first Pavilion Theatre, seen here, which opened in 1908. Beyond it, in the Alexandra Gardens, stands another entertainment venue, the Kursaal, erected in 1913. This largely glass structure lasted until 1924, when it was replaced by the Alexandra Gardens Theatre. Fire destroyed both seafront theatre buildings. The Alexandra Gardens Theatre, long converted to an amusements complex, burned down in 1993. Almost forty years earlier, in April 1954, the Pavilion (known by its post-war name 'The Ritz') caught fire as it was being refurbished for the summer season. Today, the whole appearance of the pier has altered. Extensions in the early 1930's and further reclamation in the 1970's and 1980's completely changed this end of Weymouth Bay. The modern Pavilion Theatre opened in 1960.

Weymouth Pier from the Air.

8   Since Georgian times the real attraction of Weymouth for the holidaymaker has been the fine sands and safe bathing offered by the sheltered Bay. Here, Edwardian families relax around the Jubilee Clock. These visitors would probably have arrived by rail, the Great Western and London and South Western railway companies both opening lines into the town in 1857. As rail fares became cheaper, masses of ordinary working people were able to afford a day, a weekend, a week or a fortnight at the seaside. Weymouth was to become the favourite holiday destination for the families of the workers at the GWR works at Swindon and 'Swindon Week' (later 'Swindon Fortnight') brought many thousands of visitors to the town. In 1908 the local newspaper, reporting on 'The Annual Swindon Invasion' in July, recorded the arrival during one morning of 3,121 adults and 3,050 children, all conveyed in five trains which reached Weymouth between 8.17 a.m. and 10.14 a.m.

29   WEYMOUTH. — The Sands.

9 The new visitors enjoyed the novelty of paddling and sea bathing, but they demanded more entertainment than their Georgian predecessors, who had bathed before breakfast and only used the beach for a gentle stroll later in the day. Soon the sands were alive with Punch and Judy shows, donkey rides, Pierrot troupes, jugglers and minstrels, photographers' booths and refreshment stalls. Although wealthier Victorian and Edwardian holidaymakers may have stayed in the large 'Royal Hotel', seen here, or the neighbouring 'Gloucester Hotel', much more accommodation was required and at less cost. Before long, numerous smaller hotels and boarding houses were opening up to welcome the families who wanted to be 'beside the seaside'.

10   Sand modelling has long been a tradition on Weymouth beach, the resort's fine sand being particularly suited to the craft. It is mixed only with sea water to create the sculptures which are sometimes painted for extra effect. In 1921 sand artist Swift Vincent was displaying work of considerable skill, but the next year the local council decided there were too many sand modellers on the beach - apparently not all showed the artistic merit of Mr. Vincent and by-laws were introduced to regulate their number. Today Fred Darrington is known worldwide for his skill in creating sand sculptures each summer and his grandson Mark is following the family tradition.

Swift Vincent. "Sand Artist." Weymouth, 1921.

11 Children have always enjoyed building sand castles. This little group has created a most attractive 'Seaside Villa' on Weymouth beach and it could well have been an entry in one of the sandcastle competitions held each year. A popular one at the turn of the century was the Bovril Sand Competition, which toured seaside towns and no doubt brought the firm excellent publicity since the winning sand designs had to feature the word 'Bovril' or depict the 'Bovril Bottle'.

·12  At first glance this view and the next one look strikingly similar, but closer inspection reveals that they are more than twenty years apart in date. This card dates from 1907, a year before the first Pavilion Theatre opened on the pier. At the top end of the Alexandra Gardens stands a statue of one of Weymouth's great Victorian benefactors, Sir Henry Edwards, whose gifts to the town included homes for the elderly, a Working Mens Club, and many other donations. Because of the siting of this statue, Sir Henry is sometimes associated with the presentation of the Alexandra Gardens to the people of Weymouth, but the land was in fact the gift of a wealthy Victorian visitor, George Robert Stephenson, in 1867. In 1880 the Gardens were named after Princess Alexandra of Wales – they were previously known as the 'New Gardens', which caused confusion with new gardens laid out at Greenhill around the same time. The tree-shrouded building shown behind the statue was a public convenience.

16612 ESPLANADE.                 WEYMOUTH.

13 Much widening and improvement of the Esplanade was carried out in the Twenties and this photograph shows the railings, which were added to prevent unwary visitors stepping off the prom. In the background is Weymouth's first Pavilion Theatre, opened in 1908 and destroyed by fire in 1954. In the foreground, alongside the statue, can be seen a notice board advertising the entrance charges ('entertainment tax extra') to the morning, afternoon and evening Municipal Concerts then held daily in the Alexandra Gardens. The statue of Sir Henry Edwards was unveiled in 1885. He was not a local man, but was the town's M.P. for many years and maintained his interest in Weymouth until his death in 1897. His ashes lie in Melcombe Regis cemetery, the grave marked by a 24-foot high granite column.

WEYMOUTH. Parade west showing Pavilion.

14 The Alexandra Gardens were a delight in the Edwardian era. The bandstand shown here was put up in 1891 and illuminated with fairy lights for evening concerts. Areas of deckchair seating were provided for the band's audience and immaculate flowerbeds and lawns were laid out. Thatched shelters around the perimeter of the gardens gave some protection from sea breezes and summer showers, and classical statues were added in 1904. Weymouth was criticized early in the Victorian period for its lack of public gardens, but by the end of the nineteenth century there were gardens at each end of the Esplanade and also on land in front of the Nothe Fort. This little bandstand was moved to the Nothe Gardens when the Alexandra Gardens Theatre was built in 1924, but was eventually removed from there too.

15   The bandstand in the previous photograph was to remain in the Alexandra Gardens until 1924, but from 1913 it was disguised by the erection of this large glass structure built around it. It was known as 'The Kursaal', a name taken from similar buildings in German health resorts. Its eight-sided design echoed, possibly unintentionally, the octagonal shape of Weymouth's bathing machines of the Georgian period. Resembling a large greenhouse, it provided shelter for audiences on wet and windy days, but must have been hot and humid in the sunshine. It encroached on much of the Gardens' previously open space and more was lost in 1924, when the yet larger Alexandra Gardens Theatre was built. Today an amusements complex stands on the site and there is little to be seen of 'the Gardens' of former years.

Weymouth. The Kursaal. Alexandra Gardens.

16   For a short period in the Twenties, there were three theatres in the town – The Pavilion, the Alexandra Gardens Theatre and the Jubilee Hall. In 1926 the latter was converted to a cinema and dance hall, re-opening as 'the Regent'. The new age of 'the talkies' was about to begin and television would eventually continue the erosion of live entertainment started by the film industry. The Alexandra Gardens Theatre and the Pavilion survived the Thirties together (although the Pavilion went over to showing films) and both were taken over by the military during the Second World War. It was probably doubtful if both would have continued to be viable during the whole of the 1950's, but the Pavilion (as the renamed 'Ritz') was destroyed by fire in 1954 and the Alexandra Gardens became the sole venue for summer shows until 1960, when the present Pavilion opened. Competition was then too great and the Alexandra Gardens Theatre closed in the early 1960's.

17 Complete with 'VV' monogrammed deckchairs, Val Vaux's Vaudeville Pavilion was a popular outdoor summer-season attraction on Weymouth sands. Audiences enjoyed performances by troupes of entertainers who toured the seaside resorts. When the Second World War broke out in 1939 the recreational facilities on the beach gave way to anti-invasion defences and the little theatre did not reappear in post-war years.

THE PROM AND BEACH, WEYMOUTH.

Copyright.

18 The dominant feature of a modern version of this scene would be the Jubilee Clock, but this photograph of the Esplanade was taken in the late 1860's/early 1870's and pre-dates the erection of the clock tower by some twenty years. The white house on the right is the first building in the 'Belvidere' terrace. South of it is Royal Crescent, with the King Street junction barely discernible between it and Gloucester Row. The first Royal Hotel, bow-fronted and dating from the 1770's, can be picked out in the background. It was demolished in 1891 and the present 'Royal' stands on the same site. The surface of the Esplanade appears to be in a very poor state. Perhaps some repair work was in progress, as this is obviously not a summer-season view.

19   The Jubilee Clock was originally erected on a specially-built platform on Weymouth sands opposite the end of King Street. It commemorates the 50th anniversary in 1887 of Queen Victoria's accession to the throne, although it was 1888 before it was finally finished and unveiled. The clock is a landmark and a popular meeting place and has featured on countless picture-postcard views of Weymouth over the years. In the 1920's work commenced on Esplanade-widening and the little platform was buried under tons of stone and concrete as the prom was extended seawards around the clock. Rather sombre in Edwardian days, the clock is now always repainted in lively colours which enhance the relief designs of the tower.

20   Some intrepid sightseers get a fair soaking as they watch rough seas breaking over the Esplanade extension around the Jubilee Clock. This whole area was to become the centre of much controversy in 1988, when a huge pedestrian subway was constructed at the end of King Street, but failed to provide access to the beach.

ROUGH SEA AT WEYMOUTH

21  The quarrelsome characters of the traditional Punch and Judy Show have been a popular form of outdoor theatre in England since the 17th century. This photograph dates from about 1930. The Esplanade by this date had been extended in a wide curve around the Jubilee Clock, an improvement designed to provide more space for seafront strollers, and also to stop the beach shingle north of the clock moving down on to Weymouth's most precious commodity – its wide golden sands. Today the Punch and Judy man's familiar striped booth is located at the southern end of the beach and a lively crowd gathers for every show, eager to participate in the customary rowdy humour of Mr. Punch.

22　Hedges screen the promenade from the roadway in this busy scene from the early 1900's. In the centre of the picture is one of the goat-drawn wickerwork carriages which were once a feature of the Esplanade. At the water's edge stand the large Bathing Saloons. These were introduced around 1890 and they contained cubicles, which were cheaper to hire than the individual bathing machines. A regulation distance had to be kept between the Gentlemen's Saloon and the Ladies' Saloon and the Town Council became quite concerned that proper decorum was not being observed in the use of these machines. All the problems were quickly forgotten when mixed bathing was introduced at Weymouth in the early 1900's, the local paper of 1908 stating that 'it is difficult to understand why there is so much pother about it in some seaside places'.

(Resorts such as Blackpool, Scarborough and Aberystwyth still banned mixed bathing at this date, although it was by now fairly widespread.)

Esplanade & Sands, Weymouth.

23   In the 1920's this little structure appeared on Weymouth seafront. 'Skee Ball' was very much in vogue at the time and the Skee Ball Pavilion was supported on stilts on the sands. A ball was thrown along an alley with a bump in the centre, which caused the ball to bounce high in the air and enter a target. This small amusement hall closed when the southern end of the beach became a restricted area during the Second World War and it never re-opened. The owners were asked to remove it immediately after the war ended.

Skee Ball and Pavilion Theatre, Weymouth.

24 The popularity of outdoor band concerts in the Alexandra Gardens led to the construction of a second bandstand on Weymouth seafront in the early 1900's. The site chosen was the beach opposite the Burdon Hotel (now renamed The Prince Regent). The Edwardian bandstand can be seen in this 1920's photograph. It stood first on the shingle, but people stopping to listen to the music caused considerable congestion on the promenade, which was later widened out around the bandstand. Concerts continued here until the 1930's, when it was decided to build a larger, more substantial (and controversial) structure.

Esplanade, Weymouth.

25 The Victorian bandstand's successor, the Pier Bandstand, is seen here under construction. The winning design in an architectural competition, it opened in the early summer of 1939. Art Deco in style and neon-lit, it was an attractive structure on deck, although very much a fair-weather venue. Its audience sat or danced in an area open to the skies in front of the stage, diving for cover under shelters which ran along the sides if there was a sudden shower. Many, however, felt that the short pier extending into the sea spoilt the long continuous sweep of the Bay, and the angled piles which supported it gave the structure a rather tumbledown appearance. The 'pier' section of the Pier Bandstand was demolished in 1986, the building on the Esplanade remains in use.

26  The statue of Queen Victoria stands outside St. John's Church at Greenhill and looks towards that of her grandfather, King George III, at the southern end of the seafront. Queen Victoria had no particular connection with Weymouth and her only visit to the town during more than sixty years on the throne was an unscheduled one, when the Royal Yacht encountered boisterous weather in the Channel. The statue simply commemorates a long and momentous reign and similar tributes can be found in other towns. Nevertheless, the unveiling ceremony in 1902 was an occasion of great grandeur, the late Queen's daughter, Princess Henry of Battenberg, arriving by special train to perform the honours. Sculptor George Simonds designed the statue, which is cast in bronze. The railings are long gone and the monument now stands surrounded by flowerbeds, on an island in the middle of a busy traffic system.

39  WEYMOUTH. — Queen Victoria's Statue.

27   Leading off the Esplanade, opposite the Queen Victoria statue, is William Street, at the top end of the Park District. The building on the right is St. John's School, built in 1864. It closed in 1974 when a new St. John's School opened in Coombe Avenue and the site has been redeveloped as flats. All the infant and primary schools which used to be located in and around the town centre have now closed, or moved farther out. (St. Mary's, School Street, 1824-1982; Melcombe Regis School, Westham Bridge, 1912-1970; Holy Trinity, Chapelhay, 1853-1941; St. Augustine's, Walpole Street, 1905-1964.) The building beyond the school, then the Waterloo Stores, is now The Waterloo pub.

28   A solemn procession makes its way down the Esplanade on 6 November 1921, for the dedication of Weymouth Cenotaph. There had been much discussion as to where the memorial should be sited, but a spot 'facing the sea and France' was the eventual choice. It was 'a reminder alike of the war on sea and on land – of the silent unceasing watch of the British Navy, and of the clash of mighty armies in France and Flanders, with its ghastly toll of human life'. The monument is inscribed with the names of more than 390 local men killed in the Great War. The man who released the Union Jack covering the Cenotaph at the unveiling ceremony was Albert Edward Whitby, a wounded ex-Rifleman of the Rifle Brigade, who had served in France and the Balkans.

UNVEILING OF WEYMOUTH CENOTAPH. NOV. 6TH 1921

29 'To the Glory of God and to the sacred memory of all whose names are here inscribed, this memorial is erected by public subscription from the residents of Weymouth and Melcombe Regis, in remembrance of those who answered the call of their King and Country and gave their lives in the Great War.' Weymouth Cenotaph is a 17'6" high column of Portland stone and stands on the Esplanade, opposite Victoria Terrace. The designer and sculptor was F.W. Doyle Jones. The names of 250 fallen were originally carved in the stone, but very many more names had to be added and in 1932 they were all transferred to bronze plaques on each face of the monument. In 1997, additional plaques were added to the base, bearing the names of those who died in the Second World War, and the War Memorial was rededicated at a service held on 18 May 1997.

30  Another Portland stone monument has stood on the Esplanade since 1914. Early in June that year, Mrs. Joseph Chamberlain travelled to Weymouth to unveil this pillar bearing a bronze plaque, which commemorates 16th century navigator Richard Clark, who sailed from Weymouth to join Humphrey Gilbert's expedition to Newfoundland, and John Endicott, who sailed from here in 1628 and was one of the founders and first governor of the state of Massachusetts. Mrs. Chamberlain was a direct descendant of John Endicott. She was accompanied by her stepson, Austen Chamberlain, and the ceremony was also attended by two representatives from Weymouth, Massachusetts. The Clark and Endicott Memorial originally stood in front of the old Pavilion Theatre, but it was moved in the 1960's to a site in the Alexandra Gardens. A second, more modern American Memorial stands on the seafront. Opposite the Royal Hotel, it commemorates the vast US invasion force which embarked from Weymouth in 1944 for the D-Day landings in Normandy.

31   If there was an event to celebrate in Weymouth, the traditional spot to gather was on the Esplanade, in front of the King's Statue. This open space was eventually to give way to the motor vehicle and was lost altogether in the 1950's when the present large roundabout was constructed to ease traffic congestion here. There were no such problems for the townsfolk who assembled on 24 May 1909 to celebrate Empire Day. More than 2,000 local schoolchildren and several thousand onlookers were in place by 9.20 a.m. for a short service of hymns and prayers. The children were then given the rest of the day off school – apart from twelve who had been chosen to accompany the Mayor and a party of officials as they made their way around the borough 'Beating the Bounds'. (See No. 55.)

32  The King's Statue was unveiled in 1810, to celebrate the 50th year of His Majesty's reign and to record the gratitude of the town for the fame which King George III's holidays here between 1789 and 1805 had brought to the health and pleasure resort. When this photograph was taken in the early 1900's, W.H. Smith had not yet converted the ground floor of the imposing building at the top end of St. Thomas Street. It retains its Georgian bow windows on three floors and two original front doors (the porticoed doorway to the right of the bow windows is a later addition). The statue's large plinth at this date was surrounded only by a few shrubs and railings, and painting of the statue itself in heraldic colours was not carried out until 1949.

George III Statue and Esplanade                    Weymouth

May 2nd 1904

26009

33 The top end of St. Thomas Street, an early photograph dating from the late 1860's or early 1870's. The buildings on the right can also be seen on the right-hand side of the previous picture. The photographer was William Thompson of Weymouth, who is credited with taking the first known underwater photograph. In 1856 he lowered a camera enclosed in a glass-fronted watertight box into the waters of Weymouth Bay and produced a picture of undersea life. Thompson, who practised as a solicitor in the town, was a man of many interests and a noted naturalist. He lived for a time in Frederick Place, just visible on the left-hand side of his photograph. No. 18 is another of his pictures.

34 Athletes gather at the King's Statue in 1909 for the YMCA Harriers Dorchester versus Weymouth Team Race. The background shows the altered roundhouse building, the ground floor converted to the old-fashioned windows of 'Booksellers and Librarians' W.H. Smith and Son. The firm moved into the building in 1905 and still occupies the premises today, although plate glass has now replaced the windows shown. The ground floor of the adjacent house has also been converted to a shop.

35   The area in front of the statue of King George III has long been an assembly point for buses and many services still commence at the King's Statue today, although the buses now leave from stops adjoining the Esplanade. Traffic congestion around the statue in post-war years became a real problem, solved in the mid-1950's by the construction of a large traffic island. In the 1930's the bus shelter shown was erected right in front of the Statue, possibly reflecting contemporary poor local opinion of it. There have, from time to time, been serious schemes put forward for relocating 'King George III'. Fortunately, all these were abandoned and Weymouth's prominent tribute to the prosperity brought to the town by its Royal visitor is now a Grade II listed monument.

14277. WEYMOUTH PROMENADE - JUDGES LTD.

36 A picturesque feature at the King's Statue as they waited for passengers, were the popular horse-drawn wagonettes. With trips to the local beauty spots on offer, these attractive carriages had been part of the seafront scene since Victorian times, but they were eventually ousted by motor transport. A day out in a motor coach was probably more comfortable, especially in inclement weather, but certainly less of an adventure than a trip in 'The Royal', shown here. This happy group was off to Upwey Wishing Well in the 1920's – return fare, one shilling. One or two of Weymouth's horse-drawn wagonettes survived into the 1930's.

37 Weymouth Motor Company was one of many small operators to set up after the Great War. Formed in 1919 by a syndicate of local garage proprietors and businessmen it was, considering its backing, surprisingly short-lived. Following the 1924 season, the company and its premises in Edward Street were sold to the National Omnibus and Transport Company. The NOTC later split up into smaller sections and Southern National became the local company. The chara in this photograph, FX 7322, commenced life as a lorry, the 28-seat body being fitted from an older vehicle. One of the few rules in those days was that any vehicle carrying more than twelve passengers had to have a conductor on board – not that there were fares to collect on an excursion like this, but passengers needed assistance into the quite high vehicle from a set of steps carried on the side! The conductor also described the passing scene, arranged the cream teas and collected the tips. Driver Baker and conductor Balch accompany this jolly group.

38 The very quick rise of the motor coach business after the First World War saw the formation of many small companies. Competition was fierce and business methods sometimes unscrupulous. The Road Traffic Act of 1930 brought in much tighter controls on the companies' operations and many smaller outfits disappeared from the scene. This postcard of Royal Terrace and the Gloucester and Royal Hotels was posted on 7 August 1923, and shows a long line of charabancs waiting for customers in the centre of the road in front of the King's Statue.

THE FRONT (LOOKING NORTH) WEYMOUTH.

39   Before the Second World War the toastrack-type bus was popular for seaside rides. At Weymouth, these vehicles operated services between the Pavilion Theatre and Bowleaze Cove and also ran to Sandsfoot Castle and the Nothe Gardens. Sadly, the war ended their working life and they were scrapped. Shown waiting on Weymouth seafront, near the Alexandra Gardens, is No. 2323, a Guy vehicle built in 1923. Although fun to ride in, they could be dangerous and during the 1930's a conductor was killed after falling from the vehicle.

40   This was the entrance to The Regent Theatre in St. Thomas Street with a Southern National bus ready to take everyone off on a staff outing. The single-storey entrance was a covered passageway which led into the auditorium beyond, a striking 1926 cinema transformation of the old Jubilee Hall Theatre of the 1880's. Like most cinemas, it was to undergo several name changes, ending its days as a bingo venue, before demolition in 1989. When this entrance and several adjacent properties to the north of it in St. Thomas Street were cleared, a previously 'hidden' building emerged – the 1840's 'Old Rectory' built for the incumbent of St. Mary's Church, on whose former 'front garden' the single-storey row had been built. The rectory awaits restoration and Weymouth awaits re-development of the Jubilee Hall site as a shopping precinct.

41 This was the luxurious interior of the former Jubilee Hall after Provincial Cinematograph Theatres Ltd. converted it to become the 1300-seat Regent Theatre, accommodating nine hundred picture-goers downstairs and a further four hundred in the balcony. The adjacent Regent Dance Hall also opened in 1926. Before its use as a bingo venue, the cinema was to be known as the Gaumont and later the Odeon, ending its days before demolition as the New Invicta.

42   A glance across Weymouth Backwater gives some idea of the immense size of the Jubilee Hall / Regent Theatre. The photograph probably dates from the 1930's, as Westwey Road appears to be newly completed – it opened to traffic in 1932, a long awaited 'short cut' for vehicles which had previously used Newstead Road. A great deal of reclamation was done along the western shore of the backwater to provide land for both the road and a major extension of the Weymouth gasworks. The roundabout shown at the foot of Boot Hill was part of the new road scheme. Today Westwey House, built in 1972 and greatly extended in 1996-1997, occupies much of the car park and former gasworks site at the end of Westwey Road. Paddle steamers of Cosens' fleet were a commonplace feature in Weymouth harbour at this date (the *Monarch* is in the background), but by 1967 all had gone to the scrapyard.

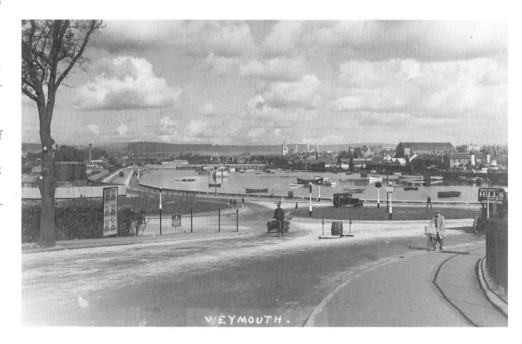

WEYMOUTH.

43  The construction of West-wey Road is shown in this view. Portland stone spoils are being tipped behind the pre-cast concrete harbour wall already in position. The stone was brought from Portland by the Sentinel DG6 steam lorries shown here – TK 3336 and TK 3337, versatile six-wheeled solid tyred vehicles owned by the Lytchett Minster contractors Newman & Masters. TK 3336 can also be seen in No. 66 at work on the construction of the 1930 Town Bridge. The Jubilee Hall is in the centre background of the photograph.

44 A 1920's view of Westham Bridge, looking towards Abbotsbury Road. Mayor Robert Bolt formally opened the new bridge on 13 July 1921 – it replaced a dilapidated wooden structure dating from the 1850's. The new bridge was in effect a dam, with sluices controlling the flow of water up and down Radipole Lake. A huge programme of reclamation then began. In the bottom left-hand corner of this photo, unseen, stood Melcombe Regis School, built in 1911 on a previously reclaimed site. At the bottom right, extensive infilling in the 1920's provided land for Melcombe Regis Gardens and Radipole Park Drive. On the opposite shore the Health Centre would be built in 1930. In the background, left, what would eventually become Westwey Road ran for about fifty yards and stopped abruptly outside the council depot – the marshy shore along here was not reclaimed and surfaced as a road to Boot Hill until 1932. Weymouth Library opened on a site in front of the trees in 1948, but the prefab building was demolished when the library moved to Great George Street in 1990 and the site is now a car park.

Westham Bridge, Weymouth.

45   A tennis match in progress on the courts in Melcombe Regis Gardens in the 1930's. Although the bowling green is still in use today (with a new pavilion), the tennis courts have given way to tarmac and this is now the car park between Commercial Road and Radipole Park Drive. The background is dominated by the tall chimney of Sunneybank Power Station, a reminder that from 1904 until nationalisation in 1947 Weymouth Corporation was responsible for the supply of electricity to the town. The western shore of Weymouth Backwater had been an industrial site since 1836, when the Weymouth Gas Works was built here and much extended in the 20th century. The large gas retort house visible at the far end of Westwey Road was demolished in 1962 and Sunneybank came down in 1974.

46 The 1930's saw the clearance of a site at the bottom of Boot Hill for the new Weymouth Fire Station of 1939, much needed as the fire brigade had formerly occupied cramped town-centre premises on the corner of St. Edmund Street and Maiden Street. Here, the houses at West Plains have been demolished and the picturesque cottages of Silver Street and Jockey's Row in the background would soon follow. Weymouth's eighteenth century town pump, in the centre of the photograph, was left in place and stood at the rear of the present Fire Station until the 1990's, when it was dismantled and re-erected in a more prominent position at the entrance of Hope Square.

47 A closer look at High West Street, seen on the right of the previous picture, although this photograph is much earlier, probably taken around 1890. The 'Old Town Hall' is a Tudor building, much restored in the Victorian period. It was from here that Weymouth's local government was administered in the days when Weymouth and Melcombe Regis were feuding with each other prior to their enforced Union in 1571. Melcombe had its own town hall across the water, where the Guildhall stands today. Note the steep drop from the pavement to the roadway outside the houses – with apparently only one street light to illuminate this hazardous stretch!

48 Old High Street on the Weymouth side of the harbour has completely disappeared from the local scene. It ran east to west behind a row of properties along North Quay, all of which were demolished in the 1960's, when the decision was made to build new Municipal Offices overlooking the inner harbour. This view looks up the street towards the Old Town Hall (not visible). The pub in the left foreground is the Weymouth Arms Inn. Repeated enemy air raids during the Second World War inflicted enormous damage all over the Chapelhay area and in post-war years many bombed houses became derelict and overgrown.

Whole streets on the higher ground above Weymouth were razed to make way for new housing developments early in the 1950's. High Street was cleared in 1961.

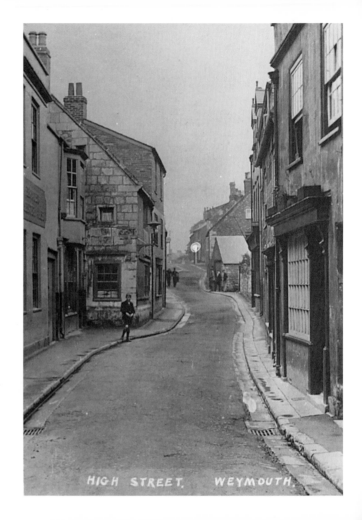

HIGH STREET. WEYMOUTH.

49 Franchise Street, Chapel-hay in about 1909. None of the terraced houses shown on the left of the photograph exist today. On the night of 17 November 1940 two parachute mines were dropped by enemy aircraft; one exploded between Chapelhay Street and Franchise Street and the houses shown took the full force of the blast. Eleven people died. The view is taken from the Boot Hill end of the street looking down towards the Chapelhay Tavern – the light-coloured building in the centre background. Chapelhay Heights, flats built in the 1950's, have replaced the bombed terrace.

FRANCHISE ST.

50  The year 1941 brought further devastation to the Chapelhay area and two severe air raids in May saw houses in Spring Gardens and neighbouring Oakley Place badly hit. Hundreds of properties at Chapelhay suffered damage in the Second World War and when blitzed streets were cleared and new houses built, some of the old street names, such as Spring Gardens, were retained. This early 1900's view shows the old Spring Gardens, an attractive terrace of houses with long front gardens, at its junction with Rodwell Avenue. 'Dora' who sent this postcard to a friend in July 1906, wrote on the back 'Isn't this a nice p.c. of Spring Gardens, its just been taken' – and indeed it is.

51 Rodwell Road, close to its junction with Rodwell Avenue, around 1909. Although the view is less leafy and rural today, some features can still be recognised. The large trees have gone, but the high pavement still runs up the hill here and the mansard-roofed cottage on the left is almost unchanged.

*Rodwell, Weymouth.*

52  Not every beach scene is a summertime one, and local photographer Edwin Seward was out and about with his camera after a winter storm, to take this picture of snow- and seaweed-covered sands around 1910, with the snowy slopes of the Nothe headland in the background. On the high ground in the centre of the picture can be seen a terrace of houses which do not exist today. These were Army Married Quarters on the Nothe and they were pulled down in 1973.

53  This postcard is entitled 'Big Guns on the Nothe, Weymouth' and the 12.5" rifled muzzle loaders had probably been there a little while, as the grass has grown up around them – although at 38 tons a piece, they no doubt made quite an impression in the turf! This was discarded artillery as these cannon had been replaced by 6" breech loaders at the Fort in 1910. As the obsolete guns were so heavy, it proved more economic to cut them up on site than attempt to haul them away.

54  In the days before the separate and rival towns of Weymouth and Melcombe Regis were officially united as one borough in the sixteenth century, the only means of crossing the harbour was by ferry-boat – the first 'Town Bridge' was not built until the 1590's. Today a trip across the water via the ferryboat which plies between the Pavilion and the Nothe Steps in the summer season, is popular with visitors and residents alike, as it was in Edwardian times. Towering in the background of this harbour scene is the great Nothe Fort of the 1860's. No longer required by the military in the mid-twentieth century, the Fort was vandalised and decaying until Weymouth Civic Society started the restoration which has transformed it into one of Weymouth's most-visited tourist attractions.

THE "NOTHE" WEYMOUTH.

55 The old custom of 'Beating the Bounds' is usually carried out on Ascension Day and is observed from time to time in Weymouth, although not on a regular basis. It is a traditional way of memorising the parish boundaries and in 1909 it was carried out on Empire Day, 24 May. The Mayor and his 'beaters', including twelve local schoolboys, needed a great deal of stamina for the day ahead. This rather tortuous route around the base of the Nothe Fort was only the first part of their perambulation of the entire borough. Various local dignitaries and the boys were 'bumped' at regular intervals to help them better remember the limits of the borough (a throwback to the days when accurate maps were scarce). Note the ladders being carried to help less able members of the party over obstacles – and carriages were supplied for the older participants who found the day's proceedings a little too strenuous!

56 'Weymouth from the Nothe', one of the most picturesque views of Weymouth Harbour. Trees frame this shot of one of the Great Western Railway Company's mail steamers in the 1930's. The *St. Helier*, *St. Julien* and *St. Patrick* of the GWR fleet all saw war service, but when the Second World War ended only the *St. Helier* and *St. Julien* returned to Weymouth. The *St. Patrick* had been dive-bombed and sunk by enemy aircraft whilst on the Fishguard-Rosslare route in 1941. A new *St. Patrick* joined the local fleet in 1948, the last ship to be built for the GWR.

57 Sandsfoot Castle is one of a series of south coast fortifications built in the reign of King Henry VIII, and was intended with its companion, the much better-preserved Portland Castle, to protect and defend shipping in Portland Roads. Sandsfoot has been falling into ruin since the seventeenth century, its decay almost inevitable as the sea gnaws away at the soft clay beneath the cliff edge on which it stands. It has always been a popular tourist attraction and the earliest guidebooks of Weymouth published in the 18th century recommended visitors to view this picturesque antiquity. The photograph shows the Tea Lawn pavilion of the 1920's. Beyond can be seen the coal hulks which were a familiar sight in Portland Harbour before the Second World War.

Sandsfoot Castle and Portland.

12242.

58 Whitehead's Torpedo Works brought industry to Wyke Regis in 1891 when it opened on a site close to the old Ferrybridge to manufacture Robert Whitehead's powerful and destructive invention. The rapid expansion of 'new' Wyke in the Portland Road area around the turn of the century was a direct result of the arrival of the Whitehead factory and Gallwey Road takes its name from the works' first manager, Captain Edwin Payne Gallwey. The postcard shows a railway siding, which linked the torpedo works to the Weymouth and Portland Railway. In later years other companies' names appeared at the works – Vickers, Wellworthy and A.E. Pistons – but all is now gone. The factory site was completely cleared in 1997 and awaits redevelopment.

TORPEDO WORKS. WYKE REGIS, NEAR WEYMOUTH.    The 'Progress' Series 133. T. H. S. & CO. B. & C

59 'Sandesfort Lane' is the title of this postcard view of the track which led from Buxton Road down to the foreshore at Wyke. Its better-known name is Rylands Lane. In this instance the name has been taken from 'Sandesfort House', the large residence on the corner of Buxton Road and Rylands Lane, which is now part of Thornlow School. Even in the late 1930's there were only a few houses in Rylands Lane, on the outer limits of the then newly-built Southlands Estate. In the early 1950's the green fields between Rylands Lane and Portland Road at Wyke began to fill with the houses of the Downclose Estate and today Rylands Lane is an urban street with houses lining both sides.

60 Back into town, via the Town Bridge. The large brick building on the right was Messrs. Hawkes Freeman's furniture store, built in 1890. It was later converted to become the Palladium Cinema, saw service as a Forces Club during the Second World War and housed Pankhurst's motor cycle showrooms in post-war years. It is now a club. The bow-windowed block on the left was demolished in the late 1920's when the Town Bridge was rebuilt, and at the lower end of St. Thomas Street the big shop in the centre of the picture – Strong and Williams, Ironmongers – came down in 1937 for proposed road widening.

On Weymouth Bridge.

61　The 1890 Hawkes Freeman building in the previous picture had replaced these old premises on the Town Bridge. The adjacent building appears in both photographs and is now the Marlborough fish restaurant. Mr. Thomas Beer Hawkes had founded his company in 1845 'across the water' in Hope Square and the business expanded rapidly in the late 19th century. A new large store built in St. Thomas Street was much extended in 1937. The company also had premises in St. Nicholas Street, St. Alban Street and West Street. Primarily 'house furnishers' they were also carpet importers, estate agents, funeral directors, cabinet makers and gas fitters. Hawkes Freeman Ltd. closed down in 1969.

62 A tranquil and almost traffic-free view of North Quay and the harbour as just one horse-drawn cart makes its way towards the Town Bridge. This was the predecessor of the present bridge. When it was demolished in the late 1920's the adjacent Town Bridge Buildings (on the left of the picture, with archways at street level) were also pulled down. Three harbourside warehouses have disappeared from the scene – those adjoining Town Bridge Buildings and the very large 'Red Warehouse' which can be seen beyond the bridge, on Custom House Quay. On the right of the photograph the buildings shown and many others along North Quay were cleared in the early 1960's to provide a site for Weymouth's Municipal Offices and its car parks.

Trinity Bridge, Weymouth. W6478.

63 The 'Red Warehouse' was once an important element of Weymouth's maritime trade. Built in the early 19th century and later enlarged, it was an imposing harbourside building standing behind the Guildhall and adjacent to the Ship Inn. It was demolished in the 1950's and this photograph was probably taken not long before its demise, as there are obvious signs of decay – windows are boarded up and roof tiles missing. The site was used for some years as a car park before the Ship Inn was extended to fill a large gap in the waterfront scene.

64  In the 1920's it was decided to replace the Town Bridge shown here (and in No. 62). This had been a substantial rebuilding in 1880 of the harbour's first stone bridge of 1824. The 1880 bridge had a central swing section which hung out over the water to allow the passage of ships up harbour, but it was very narrow. The whole structure was demolished and between 1928 and 1930 the present Town Bridge was built on the same site, a traditional one at the end of St. Thomas Street. A bridge built at the end of St. Nicholas Street in 1770 had proved unpopular and it reverted back to St. Thomas Street in 1824. During the 1920's rebuilding, a wooden footbridge was constructed opposite St. Nicholas Street for pedestrian traffic, but vehicles had to make their way into town via Newstead Road and Westham Bridge as Westwey Road was not completed until 1932.

65   His Royal Highness The Duke of York (later King George VI) opened Weymouth's present Town Bridge on 4 July 1930. It incorporates a slab of granite quarried in Weymouth, Massachusetts, and inscribed 'From Weymouth, in New England to Weymouth, in Old England, 1930'. The bridge's approaches and roadway are much wider than those of its predecessor and the navigational opening is 80 feet across. The two leaves of the central span lift to enable vessels to pass up harbour. The temporary footbridge used during rebuilding can just be seen in the background. On the right, the quay was widened in 1938 and this extension filled in the area of water shown here under the second arch of the bridge – now the stretch of road frequently flooded at times of exceptionally high tide.

THE NEW BRIDGE. WEYMOUTH.

66 Weymouth's Town Bridge of 1930 nears completion and the photograph shows a Sentinel DG6 steam lorry used during its construction. The lorry, TK 3336, was new in August 1929 and cost £1,350. The body had a capacity of 200 cubic feet and could tip three ways, end on or either side. The advance of both the petrol and diesel lorry and a sharp rise in road tax for steam-driven vehicles soon put them off the road – TK 3336 being last licensed in 1935. In the background can be seen the newly-extended Crown Hotel, the original 'Crown' building of Victorian times having been 'encapsulated' by these red brick and stone extensions of the late 1920's.

67 Cosens' paddle steamer *Majestic* making her way down Weymouth Harbour. Built in 1901 she was the largest paddle steamer to operate in the company's fleet and having a cross-channel certificate she often made excursions to Cherbourg and the Channel Islands. Unfortunately this fine vessel was lost on First World War service in the Mediterranean. The harbourside buildings in the background are little changed and the ferryman rowing his boat across the water is still a familiar sight today.

68  A variety of postcards could be bought on board the paddle steamers of Cosens' fleet. This multi-view shows the *Monarch* of 1888 which remained in the company's service until 1950. The *Majestic* of 1901 was the largest of Cosens' vessels, lost in the Mediterranean on war service in 1916. The *Emperor of India* was a second-hand vessel, having been rejected by a Southampton company when built in 1906. Despite a somewhat troubled career, she lasted until 1957, having also seen Mediterranean service in the Great War. The *Empress*, of 1879, lasted until 1955. When broken up she was the last sea-going vessel with an oscillating type engine and this has been preserved in Southampton Maritime Museum.

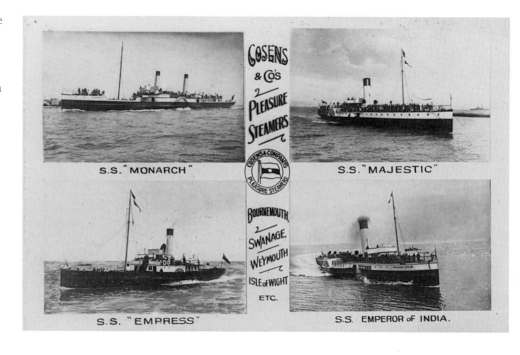

69 This view of Weymouth Pier dates from before 1908. Sailors are making their way back to the paddle steamers which will take them to the Fleet at anchor in Portland Harbour and Weymouth Bay. Cosens and Company held the contract for the liberty boats until the Great War and six of their steamers can be seen in this view. Starting from the bottom right are the *Albert Victor*, *Helper*, *Queen* and *Majestic*. Waiting at the end of the pier are the *Victoria* and *Empress*. At the pier station the stock of a boat-train is awaiting the arrival of the GWR cross-channel steamer.

70  Lulworth Cove has always been a favourite Dorset beauty spot and although just as popular today, its visitors reach it by road. Here, Edwardian passengers make their way ashore from a well-laden *Victoria* having enjoyed a more relaxing and scenic journey. The *Victoria* was at Weymouth from 1884 until 1953, when she was broken up.

Steamer at Landing Stage,

71 Summer holiday weather isn't always fine and sunny and these excursionists are well wrapped up for their sea trip along the Dorset coast. Once again, the paddle steamer is the long-serving *Victoria*. When not engaged in pleasure trips, vessels of Cosens' fleet served as liberty boats when the Fleet was in the Bay, as tugs in the days when sailing ships used the port, and they were also frequently on the scene as salvage vessels in the early years of this century when shipwrecks were a not infrequent occurrence around Weymouth and Portland. Several, including the *Victoria*, went on Second World War service, engaged in the work of contraband control in the local area, when it was vital to ascertain that ships entering the port were 'friendly' and that merchant ships were not carrying cargo likely to assist the enemy war effort.

ON THE S.S. VICTORIA

72  A view taken around 1900 and yachts both sail and steam lie under the Nothe. Across the harbour the paddle steamers *Queen* and *Albert Victor* can be seen at the landing stage. Beyond, ashore on the sands having a bottom clean, is the two-funnelled *Monarch*.

WEYMOUTH

73 Today, Weymouth Lifeboat is a familiar and vital part of the harbour scene. The town's first lifeboat was the *Agnes Harriet* which served from 1869 until 1887. She was followed by two craft bearing the same name – *Friern Watch*. The second of these was replaced by Weymouth's first motor lifeboat, the *Samuel Oakes*, in 1924 and her crew is pictured here. Tragically, two of them, the Coxswain and the Assistant Mechanic, were drowned when out in their own boat in 1926. The *Lady Kylsant* was here from 1929 until 1930, the *William and Clara Ryland* from 1930 until 1957 and the *Frank Spiller Locke* from 1957 until 1976. The present lifeboat, the *Tony Vandervell*, has been on station since 1976.

ROYAL NATIONAL LIFE-BOAT INSTITUTION.
Founded 1824.    Supported entirely by Voluntary Contributions.
60,000 Lives Rescued from Shipwreck.
The Weymouth Station.                    Established 1869.

74 Once sailing ships became embayed in the West Bay (locally and aptly known as 'Deadman's Bay') they stood no chance of escape and were inevitably driven onto the steeply shelving shingle of Chesil Beach. Bad weather forced the *Royal Adelaide* ashore near Ferrybridge in November 1872. A line was got on board and the majority of the crew and passengers were saved, but the last few were drowned as the ship began to break up. She was outward bound for Australia with an interesting mixed cargo, much of which found its way into local homes, as hundreds gathered on the beach once news of the wreck spread. Registers of the local schools show many children absent that week as they joined their parents 'treasure hunting' on the beach.

75   A stormy night grounded the steamship *Dinnington* on the unfinished Bincleaves Breakwater as she attempted to enter Portland Harbour in March 1901. This was the second stage of the enclosure of the harbour – the two breakwaters built out from Portland had been completed in 1872 and work on the second pair at Bincleaves began in the 1890's and was finished in 1905. Was the captain of the *Dinnington* aware of the extent of these works? Certainly they were not visible at high water as this picture taken the following morning at low tide indicates. There was no loss of life in the incident and the steamer was successfully refloated. The Nothe can be seen in the background.

76 Wealthy tea merchant, philanthropist and sportsman Sir Thomas Lipton was to make five unsuccessful challenges for the America's Cup between 1899 and 1930, all with yachts bearing the name *Shamrock*. His third attempt in 1903 brought *Shamrock I* (defeated in 1899) and the new *Shamrock III* to Weymouth for trial races and the incident illustrated occurred on 17 April. In squally weather a rigging screw fractured and *Shamrock III's* lofty mast came crashing down, bringing with it a huge spread of sail. Steward William Collier was knocked overboard and drowned and Sir Thomas and three other crew members were injured. *Shamrock III* was beaten in the 1903 America's Cup challenge by the USA's *Reliance*.

77   Fleet Reviews were fairly regular events in the waters of Weymouth Bay up to the outbreak of the Second World War. Naval aviation was very much to the fore as ships assembled for the royal review of 1912 and a number of naval aeroplanes and hydroplanes made flights from Lodmoor and Portland. Naval flying aces Commander C.R. Samson and Lieutenant R. Gregory thrilled the crowds who came to watch. Samson had made the first flight from the deck of a ship, and Gregory in 1912 was to take off from a ship under way, HMS Hibernia. Two famous civilian aviators, Grahame White and B.C. Hucks, also circled the fleet in their monoplanes. King George V's arrival had been delayed by fog, which continued to interrupt the week's programme, but the royal yacht Victoria and Albert arrived on 8 May to see further flights by the aircraft.

HYDROPLANE FLYING OVER ROYAL YACHT "VICTORIA AND ALBERT" AND FLEET AT WEYMOUTH, MAY, 1912.

78 Although very much a standard 'picture postcard view' of Weymouth seafront, showing the Esplanade and Royal Hotel, the real interest in this photograph lies in the motor bus passing in front of the hotel. This was a Great Western Railway vehicle, on the first motor bus service to be introduced in the town. It ran from the Spa Hotel, Radipole, through to the Wyke Hotel, Wyke Regis (now the Wyke Smugglers, on Portland Road). The service operated for four years, but was then suspended, restarting in 1912. The Royal Hotel is shown as originally built – large windows have since infilled the area each side of the main entrance at ground floor level. A narrow extension to the building now links it to the adjacent terrace at the southern end.

The Promenade and Royal Hotel, Weymouth

79 Weymouth is about the only place in the country where one could regularly meet a full-length passenger train travelling along the public road. Just over a mile long, the Weymouth Harbour Tramway links the railway station and the pier, and it ran along the harbour wall until extensive infilling was carried out in Weymouth Backwater in the 1920's. Horse-drawn when opened in 1865, the tramway first saw steam locomotives in 1880, then diesels and finally main-line trains made their way directly to the quayside. This view taken around 1930 shows locomotive No. 1331 at the end of King Street, with an up boat train. In recent years King Street roundabout has been built to the right of the picture. Use of the tramway declined after the main line was electrified in 1988. Although the long trains made slow progress through the town and held up both traffic and pedestrians, it is not only transport enthusiasts who miss the rare sight of trains which once ran through the busy streets of Weymouth.

80  The Weymouth and Portland Railway opened in 1865 and this long wooden viaduct was built to take the line across the Backwater to Littlefields at Westham. In 1909 it was replaced by a shorter iron viaduct and the area of water shown here was infilled, also providing a site for Melcombe Regis Station on the Portland line. Further reclamation in the 1920's along the harbour wall in Commercial Road made new land available for the laying out of Melcombe Regis Gardens.

THE SWANS.    *I am here all well faither*    WEYMOUTH.

8875

81 Viewed from the West-
ham shore, this photograph
shows a GWR saddle tank
train crossing the old wooden
railway viaduct in about
1900. At this date the road
bridge (on the far right) was
also timber-built and the
name of the 'New Bridge'
public house commemorates
its construction in 1859. Also
in the distance can be seen
the large sheds of Betts timber
yard. Reclamation of the area
along Commercial Road followed the construction of the
present Westham Road Bridge
in 1921, when infilling was
also carried out on the Westham side.

82 This iron viaduct spanned the Backwater from 1909 until 1976. The Weymouth and Portland Railway opened in 1865 and its last passenger train ran in 1952. Goods trains used the line until 1965 but the viaduct was redundant once the line closed. Eventually, in October 1974, demolition contractors moved in but it was early 1976 before all of the old bridge was removed. The resulting clear view up Radipole Lake had not been seen for more than one hundred years. It was not to last, as in 1987 the present 'Swannery Bridge' was completed, crossing the Backwater as part of an extensive relief road scheme, designed to ease Weymouth's traffic problems.

83   A reminder of the days when many firms made daily deliveries. This horse-drawn Co-op bread delivery cart stands outside the old gas-works in Newstead Road at the junction with Marsh Road. As well as fresh bread daily, those quick with a bucket and shovel could also obtain fresh manure for the garden!

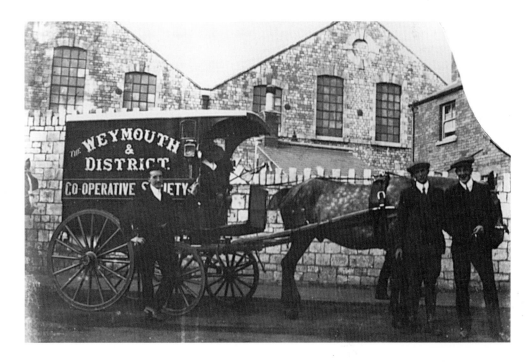

84 A pair of Great Western views. The company's railway line into the town opened in 1857, and in 1889 the GWR took over from the ailing Weymouth and Channel Islands Steam Packet Company, maintaining the regular link with Guernsey and Jersey which had begun in 1794. Familiar ships' names of the new fleet of the 1890's are the *Lynx, Antelope, Gazelle, Ibex, Roebuck* and *Reindeer*. This is the *Reindeer*, seen in Weymouth Harbour prior to the Great War, when she served in the Mediterranean. Her 1897 sister ship *Roebuck* was lost at Scapa Flow in 1915. When *Reindeer* went to the breakers yard in 1928 she was the last regular coal-fired vessel employed on the CI run. Note the beautifully painted name and crest on her stern, such a fine feature of these Victorian ships.

85 The GWR's Dean Goods No. 2467 stands outside Weymouth engine shed just after the turn of the century, one of a class of 260 locomotives built between 1883 and 1899. Designed by William Dean, they were very reliable and long-lived, the last not being withdrawn from service until the mid-1950's. So versatile and reliable were they that sixty of the class were requisitioned and sent to France during the Great War, a number returning home when hostilities ended. In the Second World War about a hundred were requisitioned and also ended up in France, one of these being No. 2467 which was renumbered WD No. 158. On the fall of France in 1940 the locos ended up in German hands and were used on the French Railways. WD No. 158 was seen shunting coaches at Lille Station in 1946 and was later sent to China under a UNRRA scheme – surely making this Weymouth's most widely-travelled engine!

86  Just off the seafront in Gloucester Street is the 'Gloucester Tap'. This part of the 'Gloucester' has no royal connections, being an entrance into the large extension built onto the original Gloucester Lodge in the 1860's, by which time King George III's holiday home had long since passed out of royal ownership and become an hotel. The line of the old royal mews can still be followed at the rear of the hotel and the Picturedrome Cinema stands on the site of the former stables of the royal household.

87  This trade card advertises 'Tilleys County Garage', which occupied a large site on the corner of Victoria Street. The striking building of 1907 housed workshops and showrooms. During the Second World War, when few private cars were on the roads due to petrol rationing, the garage was turned over to the war effort and produced aircraft parts, and on occasion the distinctive smell of 'dope', the varnish used in aeroplane manufacture, hung over the Park District. Tilleys left these premises in the early 1970's and after a spell in the ownership of Wadham Stringer, the garage closed and was demolished. An apartment block – Nightingale Court – has since filled the site.

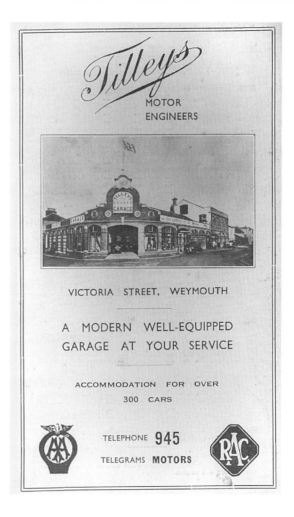

88 Just off Dorchester Road at Lodmoor Hill is Kirtleton Avenue, large Edwardian houses in a tree-lined street, when this photograph was taken in 1905. The trees have now gone, some of the houses have been extended and converted to hotels and residential homes and others have been demolished to make way for modern apartment blocks.

KIRTLETON AVENUE WEYMOUTH

The Anchorage.

89 'Sunday best' seems to be the order of the day for a sedate stroll along the Esplanade in 1911 – the ladies in the foreground are elegantly gowned and extravagantly hatted. The delightful series of little shelters on the promenade date from late in the nineteenth century and provide protection from sun or rain at intervals along the seafront. Each roof is attractively bordered with cast iron detailing. When first built each shelter had its own balcony which overlooked the beach, but esplanade extensions have left them nearly all now surrounded by tarmac. The skeletal structure bridging the roadway was a temporary frame awaiting decorations to celebrate two special occasions in the summer of 1911 – the Coronation of King George V and Queen Mary and the choice of Weymouth as the venue for the prestigious Royal Counties Agricultural Show.

Promenade & Clock Tower, Weymouth.

90 This is the 'dual-purpose' temporary arch shown in the previous photograph. Now decorated, it had welcomed visitors to the Royal Counties Agricultural Show held at the showground at Lodmoor, off Dorchester Road, from 13 to 16 June. A week later, with changed mottoes, the decorations were to celebrate the Coronation of King George V and Queen Mary on 22 June 1911.

91 Coronation Day was Thursday 22 June 1911. There was great celebration and local shops and businesses were decked out with flags and bunting, greenery and fairy lights. Thanksgiving services were held in the local churches in the morning, but a steady downpour which started at noon meant the postponement of the afternoon's outdoor events until the following day. The children assembled at the King's Statue in their 'best bonnets' must have been disappointed, but they gathered at the Lodmoor showground on 23 June for sports, entertainments and dancing, followed by a firework display. Each elementary school child in the borough was presented with a Coronation mug and a medal.

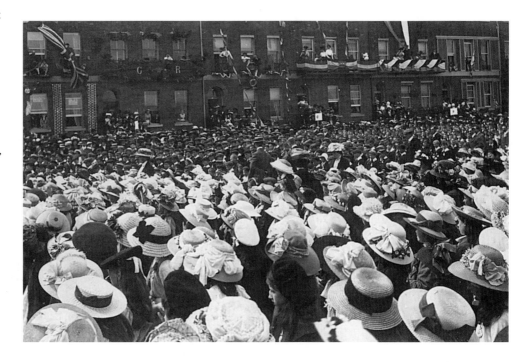

92  The 1911 Royal Counties Agricultural Show ground was on a site at Lodmoor, entered from Dorchester Road. It had been held once before in Weymouth, in 1901. Long avenues of temporary exhibition stalls advertised the wares of the leading agricultural and horticultural suppliers of the day. There were areas set aside for livestock, judging rings, marquees, refreshment tents, competition sheds and a 325-foot long grandstand. This group is passing a stall advertising a range of cane furniture.

93 The long grandstand built specially for the show overlooked the horse and cattle judging ring and could seat up to two thousand people. Huge crowds were expected to attend the four-day event and police warned the public to be on the lookout for pickpockets. Show President, Sir Everard Hambro of Milton Abbas, welcomed the Mayor of Weymouth, Councillor R.C. Watts, who formally opened the Royal Counties Show on 13 June 1911, and an evening banquet followed at the Burdon Hotel (today's Prince Regent).

94 The opening of the vast new Sailors' Home in St. Nicholas Street was a very splendid occasion in February 1907. Thousands of sailors regularly poured into Weymouth when fleet was in Portland Harbour and a facility which promoted 'health, good order and temperance' had been a long-felt need. The new building had spacious dormitories, dining rooms, reading and billiard rooms and space for dances and concerts. It was opened by the First Lord of the Admiralty, Lord Tweedmouth, who arrived with other distinguished guests in the Admiralty yacht *Enchantress*. Local architects Crickmay and Sons designed the Sailors' Home with its nautical exterior themes of ropework, dolphins and anchors and it was built by Jesty and Baker of Weymouth. Sadly surplus to requirements by 1970 the Home (by then known as the White Ensign Club) was demolished.

THE OPENING OF "SAILORS REST . WEYMOUTH.
BY LORD TWEEDMOUTH

95 There had been much discussion when the Sailors' Home opened in 1907 as to whether it should be run as a temperance institution, but there is no doubt about the theme of this photograph – it is a procession of the Weymouth Juvenile Tent No. 356 of the Independent Order of Rechabites (the Rechabites are a friendly society for total abstainers). As time goes by, with many of these Edwardian scenes it is the background which becomes the main point of interest. The onlookers are sitting on the old Town Bridge and beyond them can be seen the houses of Trinity Road.

96　A rather more solemn gathering as crowds watch the Corporation in procession following a memorial service for King Edward VII at St. Mary's Church. The King died in 1910. This is the lower end of St. Mary Street and shop blinds are drawn as a mark of respect. The building on the left is the Golden Lion Hotel. Today, plate glass has replaced most of the old-fashioned shop windows in the town, but many upper floors remain unchanged.

97  The old office of the town crier, who announced the latest local and national news on street corners, largely disappeared with the spread of newspapers in the later 18th century. The fashion for town criers now waxes and wanes, but it is largely a ceremonial post. This is Weymouth's town crier of the early 1900's. He is standing in Crescent Street and beyond the projecting sign advertising 'Chubb's Refreshment Rooms' can be seen the arcade which runs from Crescent Street through to Queen Street. This once contained a selection of small shops and stalls, but for many years, until its closure in 1996, was Digby's fruit and vegetable wholesalers.

98 St. Mary's, the parish church of Melcombe Regis, was dedicated in 1817. It was designed by local architect James Hamilton – he was responsible for many buildings in and around Georgian Weymouth, including terraces along the Esplanade and the King's Statue. This was not the first religious building on the town centre site – the first parish church which stood here lasted from 1606 until 1815, when its ceiling fell down during a service! Long before either church was built, a Dominican Friary founded in 1418 occupied a large area of land off St. Mary Street. Following the Dissolution of the Monasteries in King Henry VIII's time, the buildings gradually fell into disuse and the last remaining traces of the Friary were demolished some years ago.

99 St. Mary's Church closed in 1921 for extensive alterations and renovation work to be done and it was April 1922 before the church reopened. It was dedicated in a special ceremony by the Bishop of Salisbury and this postcard was published to commemorate the occasion. From a long list of memorial gifts, two are perhaps of special interest. The whole of the chancel work was carried out in memory of Weymouth solicitor William Bowles Barrett, who died in 1916. His assiduous collecting of local history material has been of enormous benefit to the town and historians. St. Mary's was fitted with electric lighting in memory of John and Clara Vincent 'who died together at sea 29 May 1914' – the local jeweller and his wife were among more than one thousand drowned when the *Empress of Ireland* sank in Canada's St. Lawrence Seaway, following a collision.

7 REOPENING OF ST MARY'S CHURCH. WEYMOUT BY THE R.R. BISHOP OF SALISBURY, 5.4.22.

100  The year 1914 brought an interrupted holiday for many visitors to Weymouth when war was declared on 4 August. The immediate taking over of the railways by the military left holidaymakers stranded and bewildered. Later in the month the recruitment drives began and although the initial response was poor, a great open-air meeting at the King's Statue produced a good number of volunteers. Here new recruits can be seen proceeding down St. Thomas Street. The pub on the right is the Duke of Edinburgh, and its neighbour is I.J. Brown, the optician, as today. In the background stand the four great columns of an impressive Victorian building – the Royal Baths, demolished in 1926 and replaced by the 'Clinton' building (now converted to 'Mothercare' and 'Bella Pasta' on the ground floor).

101 In October 1937 the 2nd Battalion, the Lincolnshire Regiment, relieved the Green Howards at the Verne Citadel on Portland and were given a civic welcome by both Portlanders and Weymouthians. After marching behind their band and drums from The Verne to Victoria Square, they were greeted by the Chairman of Portland Urban District Council. The soldiers then travelled by train to Weymouth, marching through the town to a second ceremonial welcome at the seafront Cenotaph. Here, large crowds watch the Lincolns march back along the Esplanade.

102  A royal visitor took tea at the Gloucester Hotel on 20 July 1923. The Prince of Wales, later King Edward VIII (and later again The Duke of Windsor) arrived at Weymouth during a West Country tour of Duchy of Cornwall property. Accompanied by the Earl of Shaftesbury, the Prince had already visited Dorchester, where he opened new Territorial Army Headquarters, met Thomas Hardy at Max Gate and viewed Maiden Castle. En route for Weymouth there was a brief stop at Upwey Wishing Well, where the waters were sampled in the traditional manner. Then on to Weymouth, where the Mayor, Councillor W.J. Gregory, and huge crowds waited to greet him. The Prince is seen leaving the 'Gloucester' on his way to the railway station and the 5.20 train back to London.

THE PRINCE OF WALES AT WEYMOUTH. 20-7-23.

103  A popular venue for afternoon tea in pre-war years was the Trocadero Restaurant, right in the heart of town on the corner of St. Mary Street and St. Alban Street. Here, a musical trio played gently in the background as patrons enjoyed cream gateaux with their freshly-brewed tea and coffee. Today the large plate glass windows of Bakers Dolphin travel agents fill this corner, but look up as you pass by to enjoy the extravagant details of the late-Victorian architecture which is above them.

THE TROCADERO RESTAURANT, ST. MARY'S STREET, WEYMOUTH.
M. WEST, PROPRIETRESS.

104  Two town centre views of Weymouth's main shopping streets by local photographer Edward Hitch (who, surprisingly, has let a printer's error slip through on this card – note the incorrect 'Weymuth'). This is St. Thomas Street and in the left foreground can be seen Lloyds Bank, which then occupied the premises which are now the National Westminster Bank. On the opposite corner stands the office of the Weymouth Waterworks Company, later to become a shop, but currently empty and awaiting a decision on the final plans for the proposed shopping centre. Across the street a builder works at a perilous and unprotected height on the shop next to the Jersey Hotel. Beyond him is V.H. Bennett's department store, its upper floors little changed today.

Weymuth  St. Thomas Street

105 Edward Hitch's photograph of St. Mary Street shows the ornate Market House which stood next to St. Mary's Church from 1855 until its demolition in 1939. In the foreground Number 50 St. Mary Street advertises free admission to what appears to be an Edwardian amusement arcade. Next door to it is Hepworth the tailor. Gosden's shop premises beside the church had replaced an ancient property on the site, which can be seen in the next picture.

Weymouth
St. Marys Church & Market

106 This very old property, dating back to Tudor times, stood on the site of the present No. 45 St. Mary Street. It was once the home of John Pitt, Mayor of Weymouth in the early 1600's. It was on the corner of Church Passage and St. Mary Street and the photograph was probably taken not long before the building was pulled down in 1883. Notice the carved human figures which support the bay windows of the old house – two of these survived the demolition and have been incorporated into the Church Passage doorway of the building which now stands on the site.

107 A walk through Church Passage and across Maiden Street leads to Governor's Lane (named after Colonel William Sydenham, Parliamentary Governor here during the 17th century English Civil War). Only the south side of Governor's Lane remains today. When the houses opposite were demolished in the early 1960's, with them went an attractive tiny terraced street which branched off it – Steward's Court. All the houses on the left of this photograph of Governor's Lane have gone and the area is now East Street car park. Those on the right remain. Beyond them can be seen the buildings of Belle Vue and Bank Buildings Baptist Church.

108 The 1930's brought a change of scene in Westham Road. The first demolitions to enable widening of this narrow thoroughfare leading to Westham Bridge and the large suburb of Westham beyond, were at its junction with the Esplanade. In 1929 the end house of Royal Terrace was removed and the rounded corner developed as Electric House. On the other side of the street the shops shown in the photograph were pulled down and the building line was set back when the present row replaced them. (Crosby's was at the junction of Westham Road and Great George Street). On the opposite corner Devenish brewers completely rebuilt the old Prince Albert Inn in half-timbered style (now renamed O'Flannigans). One business which traded in Westham Road for more than sixty years – Forte's Ice Cream Parlour, on the corner of Frederick Place – closed in 1996 and has now been converted to the Hogshead pub.

109 Weymouth lost a very distinctive town-centre building when F. W. Woolworth's cream-tiled store was demolished and replaced by a row of individual shops in the late 1980's. Woolworth's began trading in St. Mary Street in 1923 and after acquiring several adjacent properties, the company opened the completely new and much larger store shown here in July 1938. The shop blind on the left of the picture belongs to Sargeants, advertising as jewellers and silversmiths, but probably much better remembered as a pawnbroker's. The Nationwide Building Society now occupies this site. Between Sargeant's and Woolworth's ran Blockhouse Lane and this narrow passage still links St. Mary Street and New Street, taking its name from an old fortification which once stood on what is now the Esplanade.

110 Staff pose outside Biles Bros. shop in Lower Bond Street – the building has since been demolished. The local firm operated as wholesale and retail newsagents in Weymouth for many years. A placard on the left of the shop window announces 'The Times' headline 'Luxor: Closing the Tomb', dating the photograph to 1932, the year that Howard Carter's ten-year excavation of the tomb of the Egyptian boy-king Tutankhamun came to an end.

111 Numbers 119-129 Dorchester Road. This group of small houses on the Dorchester Road at Lodmoor Hill remained residential until just before the Second World War, when the first house (No. 119) was converted to a shop – a newsagent and stationer. Now the entire row is shops, the last one opening in 1948. At the rear of this terrace was a number of very small properties, 'Union Cottages', all now demolished.

112 Weymouth and District Hospital, as it appeared soon after completion in November 1902. Known originally as The Princess Christian Hospital and Sanatorium, it replaced a former sanatorium in Clarence Buildings (which was later to house Weymouth's Municipal Offices until the Borough Council moved to new premises in North Quay in 1971). The hospital was designed by local architects Crickmay and Sons and today the ground floor is almost completely obscured by modern extensions. It took its present name in 1921 on amalgamation with the Royal Hospital in School Street. Weymouth and District Hospital stands in Melcombe Avenue, which turn-of-the-century maps show as 'Bent Path Avenue'.

Princess Christian's Hospital, Weymouth.

113 Young ladies play hockey on ground adjacent to the Convent of the Sacred Hearts in Carlton Road North. This was several years before the big red brick school was erected in 1909 on a site beyond the building on the far left of the picture. The convent school closed in 1992. The main building has been converted to apartments and houses fill the former grounds. The convent house shown here has been rebuilt in the same style and converted to dwellings.

Convent of the Sacred Heart, Weymouth (*Playground*).

114 An unusual view of the old village of Radipole, taken in about 1920 from the crest of the field to the south of the village. Corfe Hill House can be seen in the distance, just above the Old Rectory. The church is just off the right-hand side of the picture.

115   Number 41 Icen Road is a view of the more modern Radipole at an early stage of development in the years prior to the First World War. The housing in the area of Icen Road, Roman Road, Spa Road, King's Road and Queen's Road belongs, in the most part, to the early years of the twentieth century.

116  Mill Street, Broadwey. These cottages still stand at the junction of Mill Street and Dorchester Road – the wall on the right-hand side encloses the churchyard of St. Nicholas Church. The postcard is postmarked 1905, but the photograph may have been taken some years previously. Could the framed prints of British Army uniforms on the outside wall of the first cottage have any connection with local celebrations when the Boer War ended? Or is there another explanation, as the pictures have a look of permanence about them?

BROADWEY 3.

117   Broadwey's Railway Station Hotel on Dorchester Road has now been converted to private housing. The two villages of Upwey and Broadwey had an initially rather confusingly named pair of railway stations. 'Upway' station, which opened on the main line in 1871, soon became 'Upwey' but was replaced by 'Upwey Junction' in 1886, which was renamed 'Upwey and Broadwey' in 1952. 'Broadway' station opened on the Abbotsbury branch line in 1885, the powers-that-be once again having selected the 'way' ending in preference to 'wey'. This led to confusion with a Broadway station in Worcestershire so it became 'Broad-wey' in 1891 – until 1913 when the station was renamed 'Upwey'! 'Upwey' on the Abbotsbury line closed to passengers in 1952, leaving only the main line 'Upwey and Broadwey'. The cottages visible beyond the pub in this photograph all still exist today.

118 A delightful scene at Upwey – 'School Time' in the early 1900's. The old village school is on the left of the photograph and Upwey children were taught here from early in the Victorian period until the school closed in 1965. Broadwey's original village school was also to close and now the whole area is served by St. Nicholas and St. Laurence Church of England Primary School, which opened in 1972. The old Upwey school building is still much used as Upwey Village Centre. The postcard is of particular local interest as it was published in the village by English's, who ran the tea rooms adjacent to the Wishing Well for many years.

SCHOOL TIME, UPWEY VILLAGE.

119 Looking down on Upwey Wishing Well halt in about 1920. The halt opened in June 1905 and was some distance from the famous attraction. A Weymouth-bound train can be seen departing and in the distance above the trees is the smoke of an up train struggling to climb the severe bank between Weymouth Station and Bincombe Tunnel, a gradient of 1/50 in places. The halt is a typical GWR construction of timber platforms and corrugated iron pagoda huts. It was rebuilt after the Second World War and closed in 1957. The railway line crosses the A354 Weymouth to Dorchester Road at a point in the centre of this photograph.

120   Building of the houses in Greenhill Terrace began in 1902 on open land to the north of Greenhill Gardens. The second block of houses which form the terrace was unfinished when this photograph was taken. The Gardens were later extended up to the first house shown here by the addition of tennis courts and putting and bowling greens. In the days before bathers were allowed to put on their swimming costumes without disappearing into the hired privacy of a bathing machine, tent or cubicle on Weymouth sands, Greenhill was the only area where gentlemen were permitted to change on the beach, behind screens. It is unusual to see bathing machines so far from the sands – perhaps these two were being used as 'changing rooms'. They are the Georgian-style octagonal type, some of which, with wheels removed, 'retired' into local back gardens as sheds and summerhouses. Beyond Greenhill Terrace the massive new Preston Beach sea defences were completed in July 1996 to solve the problems of flooding and shingle encroachment along the road here, a scheme which has also extended the promenade as far as Overcombe Corner.

Preston Beach                                              Weymouth

3rd marz - 1906

121 Remembered by all as 'Sugar-em Shorey's Cottage', this old toll house dating back to the days of the turnpike road system stood on Preston Beach Road and was home to the Shorey family for more than a hundred years. More modern photographs show the huge hoardings which later obscured this side view of the building. Mr. Shorey senior ran a horse-drawn cab in Weymouth and his favourite expression 'We sugared-em' if he beat a rival cabbie or clinched a good business deal, is said to be the origin of the family nick-name. His son, always known as 'Sugar-em Shorey', went into the log trade when motors replaced horse-drawn cabs and he and his sister delivered logs by horse and cart. In 1959 it was decided to demolish the toll house, where 73-year old Sugar-em and his 68-year old sister had spent all their lives without any modern facilities. The pair moved unhappily into a house with electricity and running water.

122 Lodmoor and Preston have long been associated with the Yeomanry and later again the Territorial Army. Here we see the Territorials in camp on the slopes adjoining Bowleaze Cove. Just above what is now known as 'Over-combe Corner' stands the row of Coastguard Cottages, complete with its signal mast. Cliff erosion caused several of these old cottages to tumble into the sea. The entire area, with the exception of the level area in the foreground, is now covered in housing.

Territorial Camp. South Western Division. Weymouth.                    Lewis Bros Bath.

123   Between the two world wars, Bowleaze Cove began to develop as an attractive bathing area away from the crowded Weymouth sands. Its popularity grew rapidly with the opening of the adjoining camp sites and caravan parks at Preston and a small café opened to supply much-needed refreshments. In 1937 a large site on the far side of the Cove would be filled by the 'Riviera Hotel', a long building of Art Deco design which now dominates this scene.

Bowleaze Cove Tea Rooms, Overcombe, Weymouth.

124 Crested postcards were much collected in the Edwardian era and here the town's coat of arms appears on one of the most popular views of Weymouth Harbour and Bay. What better way to end this collection of photographs of Weymouth and Melcombe Regis than with the description on the card itself:

*Weymouth from the Nothe. It is from this position that the best panoramic view of Weymouth may be obtained, conveying an excellent idea of the proximity of the town to the Bay and Pier, shewing also the Station of the steamers plying between this port and Jersey and Guernsey and conveying some idea of the matchless Bay of Weymouth.*